McCoy Tyner

Transcribed by Bob Leso

Front Cover Photo by Gene Martin

ISBN 0-7935-0747-2

HAL•LEONARD CORPORATION

7777 W. BLUEMOUND RD. P.O. BOX 13819 MILWAUKEE, WI 53213

McCoy Tyner · CONTENTS

BIOGRAPHY

McCoy Tyner first exploded on the scene as a part of John Coltrane's early '60s quartet, certainly one of the most innovative and influential groups in jazz history. Over the past decade he's carved a most impressive niche for himself as a composer, arranger, band leader and most significantly a pianist whose unique and forceful style has inspired and influenced a whole new generation of musicians. His impact on the music of the '70s and '80s and continuing through the '90s is comparable to Coltrane's on the music of the '60s.

McCoy was born in Philadelphia on December 11, 1938, the oldest of three children. He was encouraged to study piano by his mother. He finally began studying the piano at age 13 and within two years, music had become the focal point in his life.

In the beginning McCoy practiced on a neighbor's piano. When his family bought one, he began hosting jam sessions. Among his friends and neighbors were a number of young musicians who would go on to make their marks in jazz, such as trumpeter Lee Morgan, saxophonist Archie Shepp, pianist Bobby Timmons, and bassist Reggie Workman. "Bud and Richie Powell moved into my neighborhood. Bud was a major influence on me during my early teens. He was very dynamic." In addition, Thelonious Mond and Art Tatum were young McCoy's major influences.

McCoy, obviously a very fast learner, at age 15 led his first band, a 7 piece band that played the rhythm and blues hits. He studied at the West Philadelphia Music School and later at Granoff Music School, also in Philadelphia where he learned theory and harmony. At age 17, while playing at a local club called the Red Rooster, with a band led by trumpeter Cal Massey, also known to few close friends as "Folks", he first met John Coltrane.

Coltrane was in Philadelphia between gigs with Miles Davis. The saxophonist, whose distinctive style was still in its formative stages and whose reputation was on the rise, had no working group of his own, but secured a few engagements in and around Philadelphia, with McCoy often in his rhythm section.

McCoy later recalled that Coltrane hadn't developed the way he would later on, but "after I heard him play, I knew he was someone exceptional." The rapport between the two was so apparent, that Coltrane made it clear that he hoped to eventually have a regular band with McCoy Tyner in it.

In 1959 McCoy, who had been working mainly in and around Philadelphia, was offered his first full-time job in music with the Jazztet, a group co-led by Art Farmer and Benny Golson. McCoy stayed with the group 6 months, long enough to make his recording debut on the album *Meet The Jazztet*, but left when Coltrane finally left Miles Davis to form his own group.

The chemistry between Coltrane, Tyner and drummer Elvin Jones was immediately apparent. Coltrane went through a number of bassists before settling on Jimmy Garrison. That chemistry can be heard on the group's first recordings for Atlantic Records in 1960, which include the classic, "My Favorite Things." Coltrane was searching for ways to extend the boundaries of jazz, including a denser harmonic structure, a multi-layered approach to rhythm, and a greater reliance on scales and modes as a basis for improvisation, and McCoy was right there with him.

The pianist participated in numerous historical recording sessions with Coltrane, including *Africa Brass*, *A Love Supreme*, and *Ascension*, to name a few, during his six year tenure with the quartet. He also began recording on his own, occasionally in a trio context (his first album was *Inception*, recorded in 1962 for Impulse, which had become Coltrane's label), and tended toward a somewhat more melodic and conservative approach than he displayed in the context of Coltrane's group.

As close as his musical relationship with Coltrane was, it was inevitable that McCoy would eventually want to form his own group. His split from his mentor, which was an amicable one, was hastened by the fact that Coltrane, whose music was moving in an increasingly free-form direction, had added a second saxophonist (Pharoah Sanders) and a second drummer (Rashid Ali). McCoy was simply having difficulty hearing himself play.

Unfortunately, for the next few years, he encountered difficulty making a living playing his music. He continued to record as a leader, making a series of impressive albums for the Blue Note label, and he worked as a sideman with the great Art Blakey and his Jazz Messengers. It took McCoy several years to establish himself as a leader.

In 1971 McCoy signed a recording contract with Milestone Records, at which time things began to improve. His first album for the label, *Sahara*, released the following year, received two Grammy nominations and was named "Album Of The Year" in the Down Beat Critics Poll. Subsequent LP's for the label found him stretching out in a wide variety of musical contexts. He recorded with strings, with large horn sections, with voices; with all-star ensembles, with tightly-knit trios, and solo; in clubs, in concert, and in the studio. In '78 he teamed with Sonny Rollins, Ron Carter and Al Foster to tour the U.S. as the Milestone Jazzstars. The tour, documented on a live double LP set, was one of the most extensively-promoted *ever* by an acoustic jazz ensemble.

Throughout the '70s, his art and influence continued to grow. His readily identifiable piano style – forceful, percussive, dense, but also capable of tender lyricism – came more clearly into focus. So did his influence; there are few jazz pianists on the scene today, including the veterans, whose styles have not in some way been touched by his. This influence has been felt also in the contributions of the many outstanding musicians who have gained valuable schooling as members of his band, such as the late Woody Shaw, Sonny Fortune, Alphonse Mouzon, Azar Lawrence, Gary Bartz, George Adams, Joe Ford, John Blake, Benny Maupin, and Guilherme Franco to name a few. McCoy's dedication to the acoustic piano and refusal to convert to electricity has been an inspiration to many.

The worldwide awards and accolades are too numerous to list. Suffice to say that he is recognized by musicians, critics and listeners alike as a major force of the '60s, '70s, '80s and now the '90s.

FOLKS

By McCOY TYNER

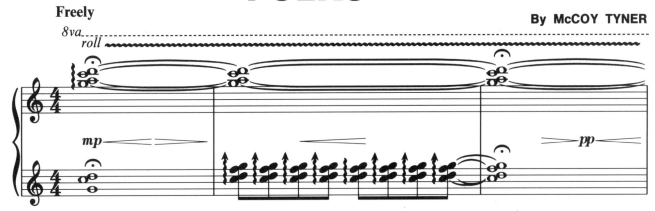

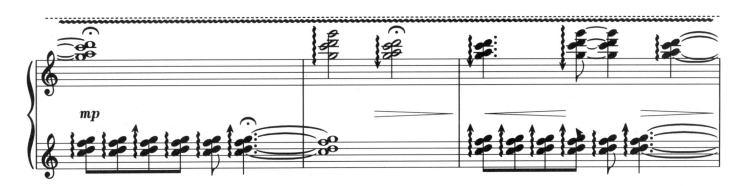

A Rubato

Solo: 1st Chorus

G **Rubato**
3rd Chorus

20

FLY WITH THE WIND

By McCOY TYNER

FOR TOMORROW

Moderate Jazz Waltz

(♫ played as ♩³♪)

By McCOY TYNER

HIGH PRIEST

Moderate Swing

By McCOY TYNER

I 4th Chorus

D.C. al Fine
(take both endings)

ISLAND BIRDIE

Bright Calypso Tempo
(Intro played once on D.C.)

By McCOY TYNER

A *(Melody played by steel drum and alto sax)*

N Additonal Chorus

JUST IN TIME

Moderately Fast Swing

Words by BETTY COMDEN and ADOLPH GREEN
Music by JULE STYNE

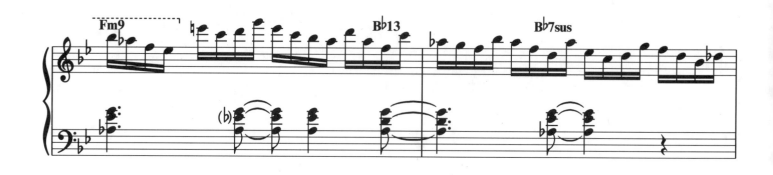

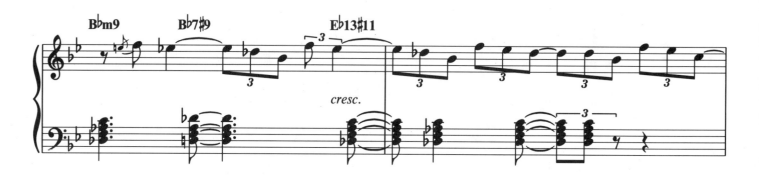

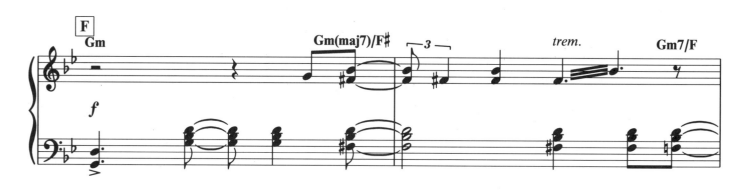

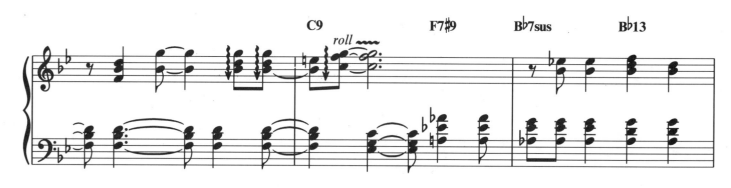

LA HABANA SOL
(The Havana Sun)

Moderately, Latin Feel

(Played by ensemble)

By McCOY TYNER

MAN FROM TANGANYIKA

By McCOY TYNER

African feel (12/8 feel)

A *(Melody played by flute and piano)*

THEME FOR NANA

A **Slowly**

(Melody played by flute)

By McCOY TYNER

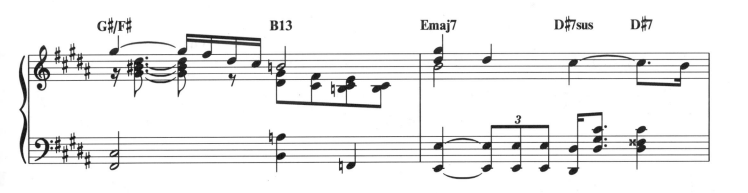

Double-time swing feel

PRELUDE TO A KISS

By DUKE ELLINGTON
IRVING GORDON and IRVING MILLS

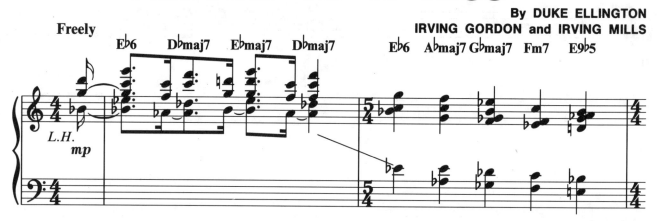

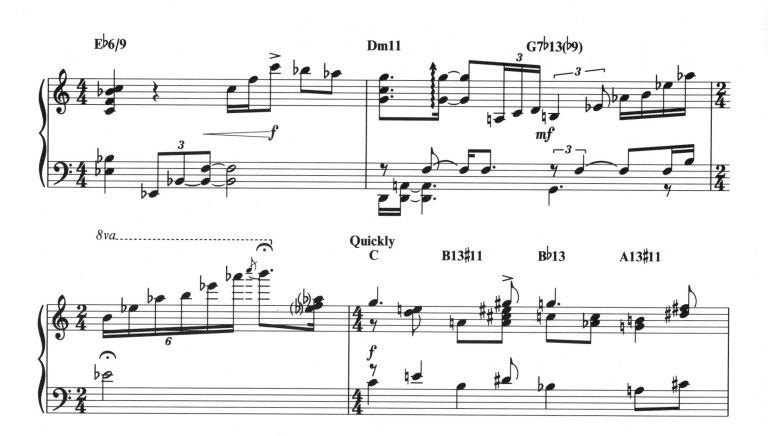

YOU STEPPED OUT OF A DREAM

Words by GUS KAHN
Music by NACIO HERB BROWN

Moderately

SEÑOR CARLOS

By McCOY TYNER

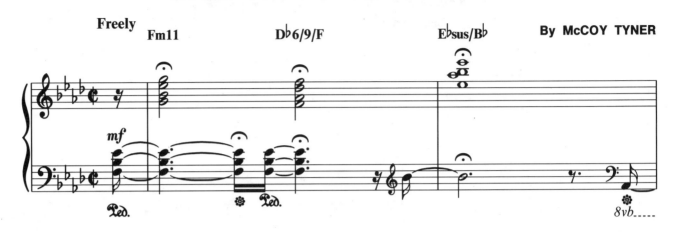

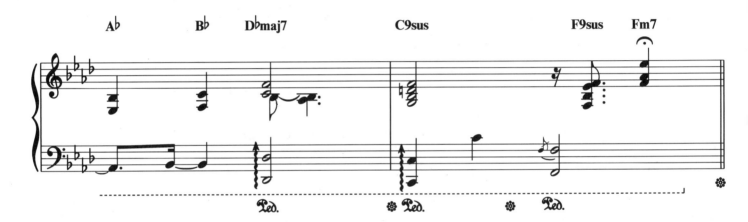

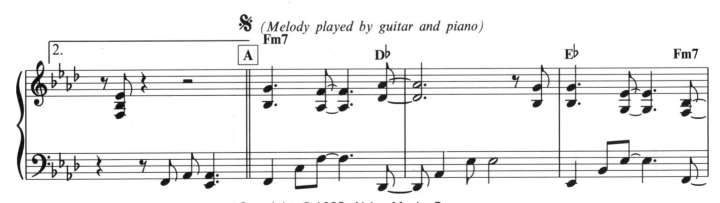